TEACHER
Coloring Book

A HUMOROUS, SNARKY & UNIQUE ADULT COLORING BOOK FOR TEACHERS FOR STRESS RELIEF AND RELAXATION

PUBLISHED BY THE FRUITFUL MIND LTD.

Disclaimer

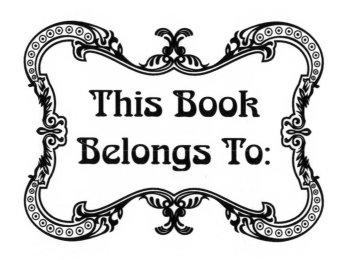

This Book
Belongs To:

BONUS

Relax And Create Your Own Masterpiece With
THIS 10 PAGE FREE *Beautiful Adult Coloring Book*

Claim Your FREE Coloring Book at:

www.freecoloringbooklet.com

Samples Below

"It's been a long week"

~ Me, in the middle of Tuesday.

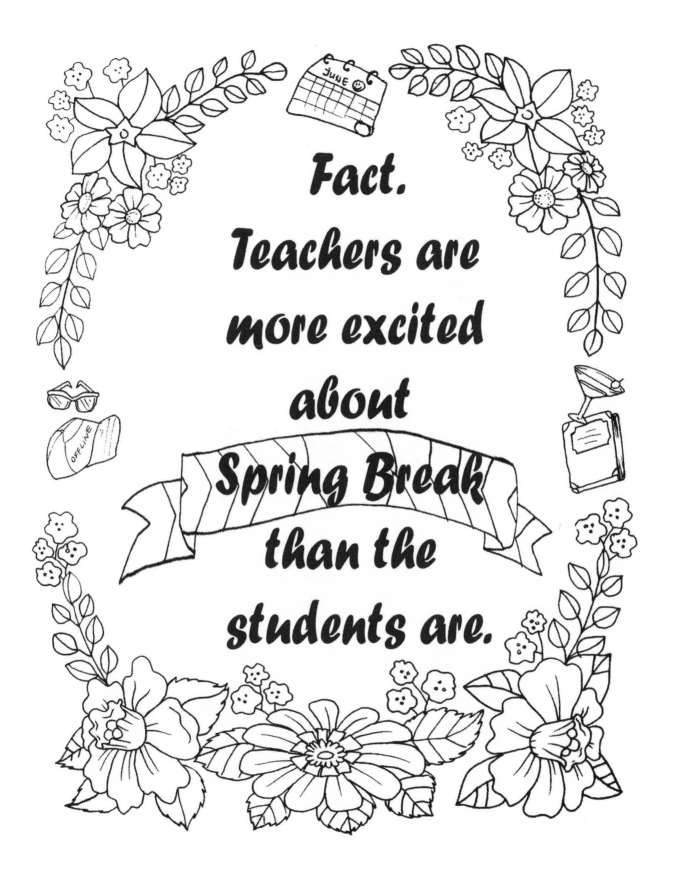

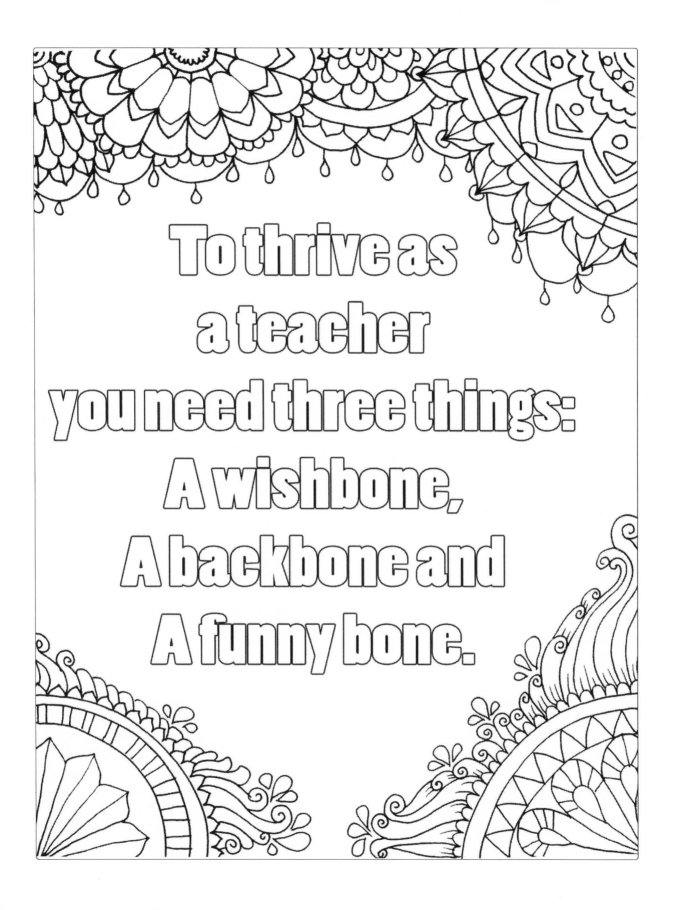

Smonday:
the moment when Sunday
stops feeling like a Sunday
and the anxiety of
Monday kicks in.

Pinning teaching ideas should get you some kind of professional development credit.

"Stop licking the window"
(Things you'd never thought
you'd have to say)
#TeachersLife

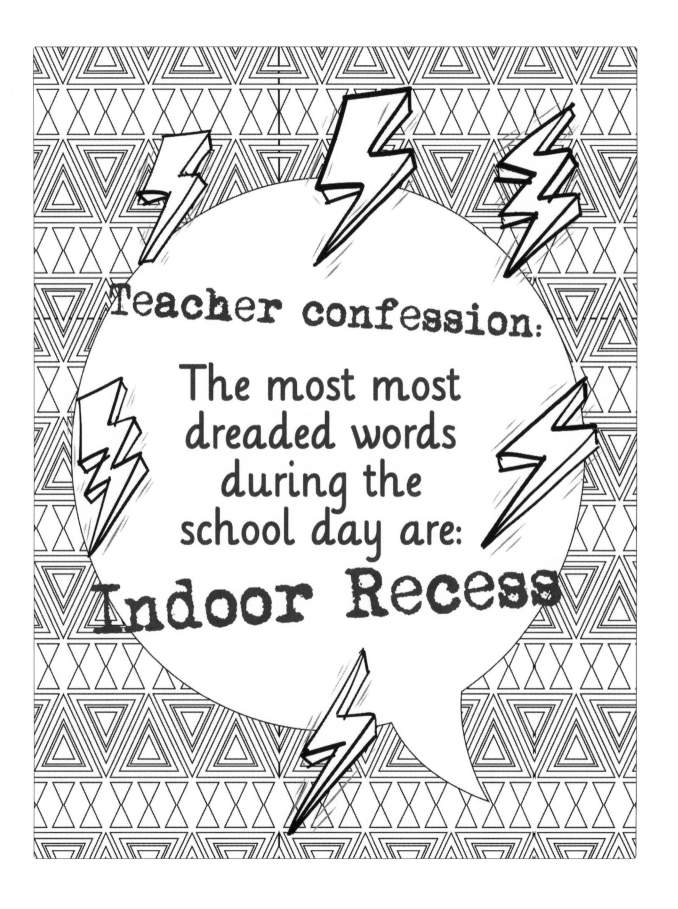

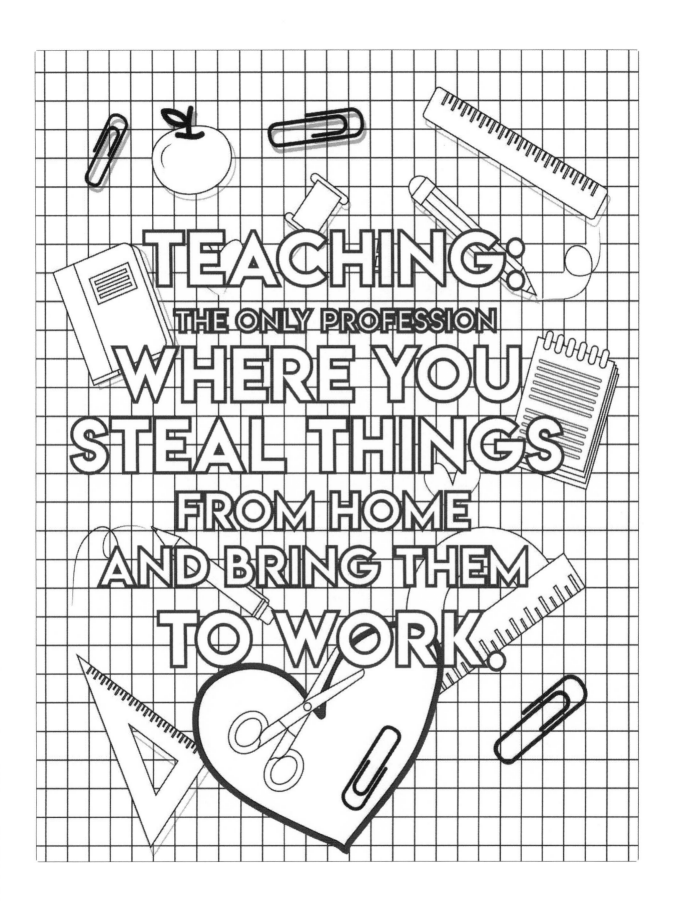

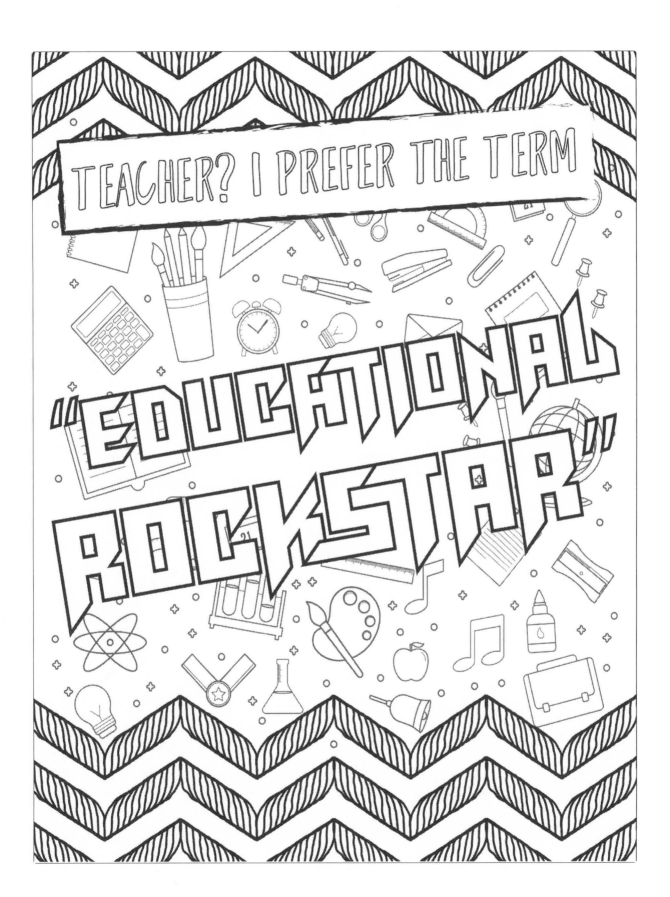

Made in the USA
Middletown, DE
05 December 2018